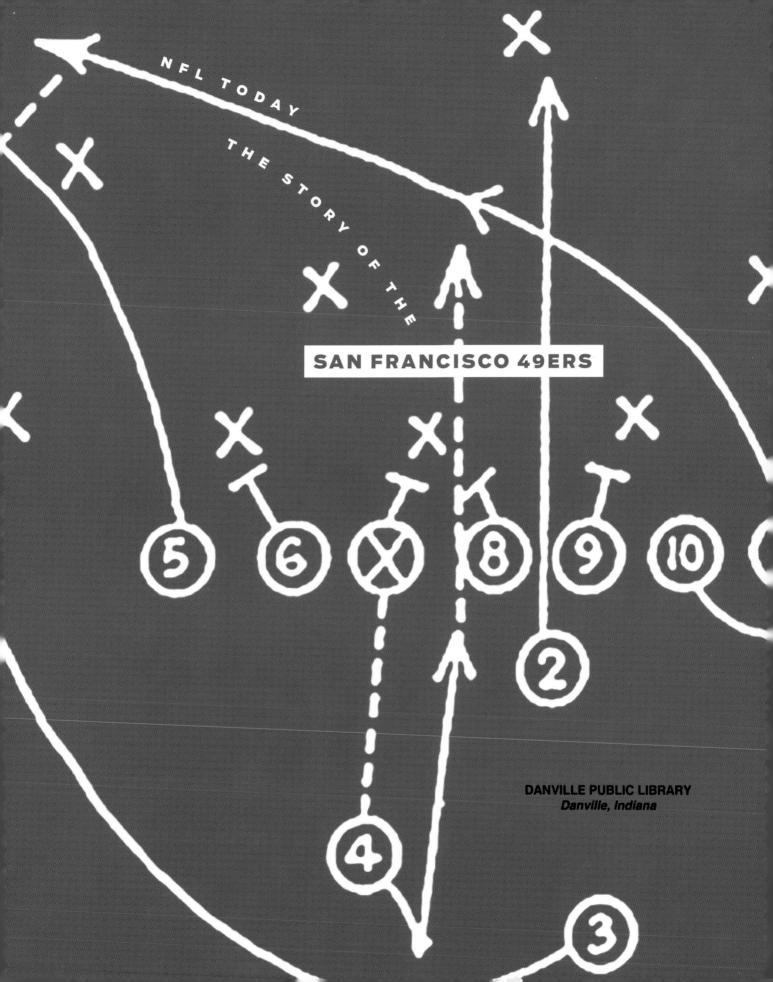

NFL TODAY

THE STORY OF THE

SAN FRANCISCO 49ERS

NFL TODAY

THE STORY OF THE SAN FRANCISCO 49ERS

JIM WHITING

CREATIVE EDUCATION

PUBLISHED BY CREATIVE EDUCATION
P.O. BOX 227, MANKATO, MINNESOTA 56002
CREATIVE EDUCATION IS AN IMPRINT OF THE CREATIVE COMPANY
WWW.THECREATIVECOMPANY.US

DESIGN AND PRODUCTION BY BLUE DESIGN
ART DIRECTION BY RITA MARSHALL
PRINTED IN THE UNITED STATES OF AMERICA

PHOTOGRAPHS BY CORBIS (BETTMANN, MICHAEL
MACOR/SAN FRANCISCO CHRONICLE), GETTY IMAGES
(BRIAN BAHR, ROBERT BECK/SPORTS ILLUSTRATED,
JOHN BIEVER/SPORTS ILLUSTRATED, ROY DABNER/
AFP, GEORGE GOJKOVICH, OTTO GREULE JR., OTTO
GREULE JR./ALLSPORT, LEON HALIP, ANDY HAYT,
THEARON W. HENDERSON, WALTER IOOSS JR./
SPORTS ILLUSTRATED, JED JACOBSOHN, HEINZ
KLUETMEIER/SPORTS ILLUSTRATED, KIRBY LEE/NFL,
RONALD MARTINEZ/ALLSPORT, PETER READ MILLER/
SPORTS ILLUSTRATED, MPS/NFL, DOUG PENSINGER/
ALLSPORT, ROBERT RIGER, FRANK RIPPON/NFL,
GEORGE ROSE, PAUL SPINELLI, KEVIN TERRELL,
TRAVEL INK, GREG TROTT, MICHAEL ZAGARIS,
MICHAEL ZAGARIS/SAN FRANCISCO 49ERS)

LIBRARY OF CONGRESS CATALOGING-IN-PUBLICATION DATA
WHITING, JIM.
THE STORY OF THE SAN FRANCISCO 49ERS / BY JIM WHITING.
P. CM. — (NFL TODAY)
INCLUDES INDEX.
SUMMARY: THE HISTORY OF THE NATIONAL FOOTBALL LEAGUE'S
SAN FRANCISCO 49ERS, SURVEYING THE FRANCHISE'S BIGGEST
STARS AND MOST MEMORABLE MOMENTS FROM ITS INAUGURAL
SEASON IN 1946 TO TODAY.
ISBN 978-1-60818-319-7
1. SAN FRANCISCO 49ERS (FOOTBALL TEAM)—HISTORY—JUVENILE
LITERATURE. I. TITLE.

GV956.S3W55 2013
796.332'640979461—DC23   2012033817

FIRST EDITION
9 8 7 6 5 4 3 2 1

COVER: QUARTERBACK COLIN KAEPERNICK
PAGE 2: RUNNING BACK FRANK GORE
PAGES 4–5: DEFENSIVE END FRED DEAN
PAGE 6: QUARTERBACK JOE MONTANA

TABLE OF CONTENTS

A Bay Area Beginning

The discovery of gold in central California in 1848 transformed the sleepy town of San Francisco into the largest city on the West Coast. Devastated by an earthquake in 1906, San Francisco emerged even stronger and became the principal port of embarkation for troops and warships in the Pacific Theater during World War II. Today, "The City" (as many residents call it) is California's fourth-largest city and one of the top tourist destinations in the world. Its spectacular waterfront, Golden Gate Bridge, Chinatown district, cable cars, and colorfully painted Victorian-era houses are just a few of its many defining attractions.

Some of those tourists join local football fans to cheer on San Francisco's professional football team, the 49ers, named after the thousands of miners who raced to California in 1849 during the gold rush. In the early 1940s, trucking company executive Anthony Morabito envisioned pro football in San Francisco. However, the National Football League (NFL) denied his request to join the league. The league didn't

SPEEDY BACK LEN ESHMONT SCORED THE FIRST TOUCHDOWN FOR THE 49ERS

Leo Nomellini

DEFENSIVE TACKLE / 49ERS SEASONS: 1950–63 / HEIGHT: 6-FOOT-3 / WEIGHT: 259 POUNDS

Leo Nomellini was the first player the 49ers drafted after joining the NFL. In high school, Nomellini had no idea he would end up playing professional football. Born in Italy, Nomellini moved with his family to Chicago, Illinois, when he was a baby. As a teen, he worked to help support his family and had no time for high school sports. He began playing football after joining the Marine Corps in Cherry Point, North Carolina, and he went on to a successful college football career at the University of Minnesota. As a member of the 49ers, "The Lion" displayed rare agility, speed, and aggression throughout 174 consecutive regular-season games. One of the best pass rushers in the league, Nomellini was also versatile. The 49ers faced a crisis in 1955 when many of their players went down with injuries. To compensate for the shortage, Nomellini played tackle on both sides of the line, with little time for breathers. "He was as strong as three bulls," said Joe Perry, a 49ers running back in the 1950s. "He'd slap you on the back and knock you 20 feet."

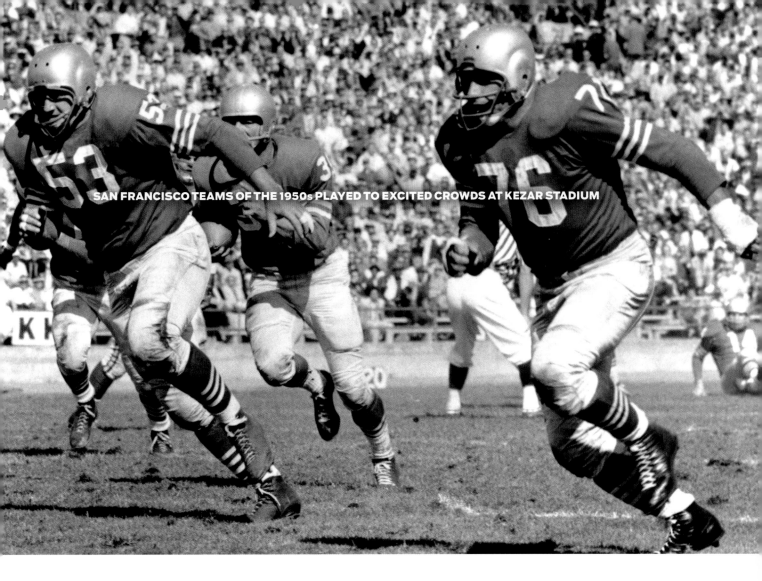
SAN FRANCISCO TEAMS OF THE 1950s PLAYED TO EXCITED CROWDS AT KEZAR STADIUM

have any teams west of Chicago and were satisfied with keeping things that way. So, Morabito and his brother, Victor, founded the 49ers as part of the All-America Football Conference (AAFC) in 1946.

The 49ers' first coach, Lawrence "Buck" Shaw, assembled a talented lineup that included quarterback Frankie Albert, running back and defensive back Len Eshmont, and guard Bruno Banducci. The 49ers put together a combined record of 38–14–2 before the AAFC folded after the 1949 season. Unfortunately, the Cleveland Browns were even better, losing just four games in four years and winning the league championship each year.

The NFL, having changed its stance on westward expansion, absorbed the 49ers and two other teams—the Browns and Baltimore Colts—in 1950. From 1951 to 1954, the 49ers posted winning records behind star players such as defensive tackle Leo Nomellini and Hardy Brown, a small but ferocious linebacker.

"How about we call it the shotgun?"

COACH "RED" HICKEY ON NAMING A
NEW OFFENSIVE FORMATION

Hugh "The King" McElhenny and Joe "The Jet" Perry emerged as star running backs for San Francisco in the early 1950s. Albert had such confidence in McElhenny that he convinced Coach Shaw to put the rookie into a preseason game even though McElhenny had just reported to training camp and didn't know the plays or even his teammates' names. McElhenny took a pitch from Albert and ran 42 yards for a touchdown. Albert also helped give Perry his nickname when the quarterback commented, "When that guy comes by to take a handoff, his slipstream darn near knocks you over. He's strictly jet-propelled." In 1953 and 1954, The Jet became the first player to rush for more than 1,000 yards in back-to-back seasons. By then, Y. A. Tittle was San Francisco's quarterback. Fans called him, McElhenny, Perry, and running back John Henry Johnson the "Million Dollar Backfield."

Tittle also had a standout receiver in former basketball star R. C. Owens. The quarterback often threw "alley-oop" passes to Owens, who would jump as high as he needed to grab the ball. "It's the strangest thing I've ever seen on a football field," one reporter noted. Gordie Soltau was another key contributor. The wide receiver was also the team's placekicker and made three Pro Bowl appearances.

Still another vital cog in the team's 1950s success was offensive tackle and defensive end Bob St. Clair, a five-time Pro-Bowler who, at 6-foot-9, was the league's tallest player. The San Francisco native was nicknamed the "King of Kezar," because he played so many high school, college, and pro games in Kezar Stadium, the 49ers' home field until they moved to Candlestick Park in 1971.

In 1957, rookie quarterback John Brodie displayed his potential when he filled in for the injured Tittle in a game against the mighty Colts. With less than a minute left, Brodie threw the game-winning touchdown pass to McElhenny. Under Frankie Albert, now the team's coach, the 49ers went 8–4 on the season and made their first trip to the NFL playoffs, losing to the Detroit Lions, 31–27.

The 1960s were tumultuous years for San Francisco. While they often had respectable records, the

The Shotgun Blasts Off

During a mediocre 1960 season, 49ers head coach Howard "Red" Hickey decided to spice up the team's offense by implementing a new formation. Hickey felt that defenses had decoded every offensive play, so a new formation would catch them off-guard. The coach combined elements from several different strategies, calling his formation the "shotgun" because it sprayed receivers all over the field. "I'm an old country boy, and I used to go hunting with a shotgun," Hickey said. "How about we call it the shotgun?" In this formation, the quarterback lined up several yards behind the center, and the center snapped the ball back into his waiting hands. Running backs lined up behind but parallel to the tackles, which helped stop pass rushers and gave the quarterback more time to view the field. The 49ers introduced their new setup on November 27, 1960, in a game against the powerful Baltimore Colts and stunned their opponents with a 30–22 upset. San Francisco went on to win three of its last four games that season by using the shotgun offense.

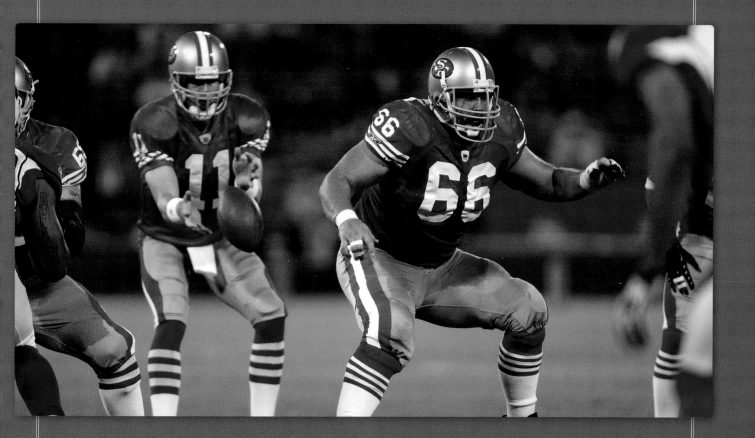

THE 49ERS CONTINUED TO RUN THE SHOTGUN OFFENSE WITH QUARTERBACK ALEX SMITH

PROTECTIVE DEFENDERS ALLOWED JOHN BRODIE TO LAST 16 SEASONS IN SAN FRANCISCO

49ers never reached the playoffs. That decade featured the advent of the "shotgun" formation. San Francisco head coach Howard "Red" Hickey introduced the formation near the end of the 1960 season. For the shotgun to work, the quarterback had to be able to scramble for yardage, and Brodie, more mobile than Tittle, became the team's primary starter. "I held John off until the shotgun," Tittle later admitted.

Hickey further confused opponents by rotating quarterbacks. When Brodie was not in the game, Hickey used Billy Kilmer. In 1961, Kilmer passed for a modest 286 yards but rushed for a whopping 509. He scored a team-record four rushing touchdowns in one game against the Minnesota Vikings.

Hugh McElhenny

RUNNING BACK / 49ERS SEASONS: 1952–60 / HEIGHT: 6-FOOT-1 / WEIGHT: 195 POUNDS

After graduating from high school, Hugh McElhenny received a call from Los Angeles Rams assistant coach Hamp Pool. Pool asked if McElhenny wanted to play for the Rams, but McElhenny's father declined, sending his son to play at the University of Washington instead. When he finished, the young McElhenny headed to the NFL Draft, expecting to be chosen by the Rams. However, the Rams used their first pick to select quarterback Billy Wade, and the 49ers snapped up McElhenny before the Rams could choose again. McElhenny had an immediate impact on the league, using his breakaway speed to record the best rushing average (seven yards per carry) in the NFL in 1952 and earning Rookie of the Year honors. Dubbed "The King" by 49ers quarterback Frankie Albert, McElhenny ran with a distinctive style characterized by long strides and high knee action. He also had rare shiftiness in the open field, which contributed to an 89-yard run from scrimmage during his rookie season. "He could change direction on a dime," said 49ers offensive end Billy Wilson. "He had great cutting ability where other backs were just slashers."

The Gold Rush of 1976

Today, the 49ers' "Gold Rush" refers to the team's cheerleading squad, but the term meant something completely different almost four decades ago. The 49ers struck gold in the mid-1970s when a talented group of defensive linemen came together for a record-setting season. Tommy Hart and Cedrick Hardman manned the defensive ends, while Cleveland Elam and Jimmy Webb played the tackle spots. During the games when Hardman sat out with a broken leg, end Tony Cline filled in, and Bill Cooke also lent a hand at any position as needed. This defensive unit earned the nickname "Gold Rush." In 1976, the Gold Rush was a defensive wall, helping to limit opposing offenses to a scant 13 passing touchdowns for the year. On the season, the 49ers allowed an average of only 13.6 points per game and set a team record with 61 quarterback sacks. The team's most exhilarating game of 1976 came against the Los Angeles Rams, who were undefeated and heavily favored. Surprising everyone, the 49ers shut out the Rams 16–0, sacking quarterback James Harris 10 times in the process.

Coach Walsh and Joe Cool

By the end of the '60s, the 49ers had stocked up on new talent. Brodie and wide receiver Gene Washington led the offense, while linebacker Dave Wilcox and cornerback Jimmy Johnson anchored a solid defense. In 1968, Dick Nolan took over as coach. During his first year, the team produced a 7–6–1 record. San Francisco really seemed to turn a corner in 1970, when it went 10–3–1. The 49ers reached the playoffs in 1970, 1971, and 1972, but the Dallas Cowboys knocked them out each time.

The 49ers' strong seasons of the early '70s were followed by several years of frustration. Powered by a solid defensive unit, the 49ers finished 8–6 in 1976. Aside from that one bright spot, however, the franchise failed to produce a winning record for the remainder of the decade.

From 1976 to 1978, San Francisco tried four head coaches

THE 49ERS FOUND A WINNING COMBO IN QUARTERBACK JOE MONTANA AND COACH BILL WALSH

Bill Walsh

COACH / **49ERS SEASONS: 1979–88**

When Bill Walsh was hired as head coach of the 49ers in 1979, the team was in a severe slump. Walsh, who had been an assistant coach for the Oakland Raiders, Cincinnati Bengals, and San Diego Chargers, quickly rebuilt the team. After just three years, he led the 49ers to their first Super Bowl victory, and the success didn't stop there. Under Walsh's direction, the 49ers won six NFC West Division titles and three Super Bowls, making the 49ers the "Team of the '80s." Walsh possessed an uncanny ability to evaluate and develop players' talent, and he is credited with helping several star quarterbacks—including 49ers great Joe Montana, Ken Anderson of the Bengals, and Dan Fouts of the Chargers—fulfill their potential. Walsh was one of the first coaches to preplan series of plays in the office during the week instead of making decisions during the chaos of the game. "When we go over the game plan during the week, it doesn't look like it will work," Montana once said. "But when we get into the game and use it, it seems that the plan always works."

"It seems that the plan always works."

JOE MONTANA ON BILL WALSH'S GAME PLANS

before bringing in Bill Walsh, who had a reputation as a great offensive mind. "When I took over the 49ers, we were acknowledged as the least-talented, least-experienced franchise in the NFL," Walsh later noted. In Walsh's first season in San Francisco, the 49ers' offense revolved around quarterback Steve DeBerg. The 49ers selected quarterback Joe Montana in the third round of the 1979 NFL Draft and took a year to groom the rookie before inserting him into the lineup.

With Montana at the helm, the 49ers opened the 1980 season with three straight wins. They also made national headlines late in the season when they overcame a 35–7 halftime deficit against the New Orleans Saints. San Francisco scored 31 unanswered points that day to win 38–35 in overtime in what was then the biggest comeback in NFL history.

ithin three years of his hiring, Walsh had assembled a star-studded team that included Montana, receiver Dwight Clark, and safety Ronnie Lott. The roster also included veteran linebacker Jack "Hacksaw" Reynolds, who had earned his nickname in college when he used a hacksaw to cut a car in half. Walsh noted that the nickname also fit Reynolds's playing style, "because he cut people down."

In two years, the 49ers went from worst to first, jumping from 2–14 in 1979 to 13–3 in 1981. They claimed the National Football Conference (NFC) West Division title for the first time since 1972, then beat the Cowboys for the NFC championship. In Super Bowl XVI against the Cincinnati Bengals, the 49ers led 20–0 at halftime. Walsh encouraged his players to stay focused. "I wasn't comfortable with the lead," he said later. "Maybe if it had been 24–0, the Bengals might have caved in, but not with the score 20–0." Although the Bengals came back with three touchdowns, the 49ers booted two field goals and held on to win 26–21. After 31 seasons, the 49ers were world champions.

The following season was a letdown, marred by injuries and an NFL players' strike that shortened the schedule. The 49ers came back strong in 1983, finishing 10–6 and winning the NFC West again. The Washington Redskins knocked them off in the playoffs, but the 49ers were about to go on a tear. Before

The Catch

When the 49ers went 13–3 in 1981 and showed signs of greatness, they did not feel much respect from other teams. The 49ers had been a bad team in the late '70s, and a growing rivalry with the Dallas Cowboys didn't help. In 1980, the Cowboys had crushed San Francisco 59–14. The 49ers returned the favor in 1981 with a 45–14 win, but many Dallas players suggested that the "real" Cowboys hadn't shown up. But the 49ers continued to play well and drove to the 1981 NFC Championship Game, where they faced the Cowboys. With only 58 seconds left in the game, the Cowboys led 27–21. San Francisco had the ball on Dallas's six-yard line. Quarterback Joe Montana tossed what appeared to be a high, throwaway pass. It was actually a carefully planned play called "Sprint Right Option." In the back of the end zone, San Francisco wide receiver Dwight Clark soared impossibly high and snared the ball, giving the 49ers the victory. "The Catch," as the play is now known, propelled the 49ers to the first of four Super Bowl wins during the 1980s.

JOE MONTANA DID NOT SEE DWIGHT CLARK CATCH THE BALL BUT HEARD THE CROWD SCREAM

JACK REYNOLDS MOWED DOWN THE OPPOSITION TO STOP THE BALL

IN HIS STELLAR 1985 SEASON, ROGER CRAIG LED THE NFL WITH 92 RECEPTIONS

the end of the decade, San Francisco would win three more Super Bowls—beating the Miami Dolphins 38–16 in Super Bowl XIX, the Bengals 20–16 in Super Bowl XXIII, and the Denver Broncos 55–10 in Super Bowl XXIV.

Two-time NFL Most Valuable Player (MVP) Montana received much of the credit for this dynasty. But Montana didn't win the Super Bowls alone. He was surrounded by players such as tough running back Roger Craig and smooth receiver Jerry Rice. In 1985, Craig became the first player in league history to amass 1,000 yards rushing and 1,000 yards receiving in a season. During the last half of the 1980s, Rice emerged as a top-notch receiver; even before he ended his career, many people considered him to be the best receiver in NFL history. Walsh retired as head coach early in 1989 after the 49ers won their third Super Bowl.

Assistant coach George Seifert replaced Walsh. Under Seifert, Montana enjoyed the best season of his career in 1989, passing for 3,521 yards and 26 touchdowns. The 49ers barreled to their second consecutive Super Bowl, crushing the Broncos by 45 points. Montana had such a spectacular day, tossing five touchdown passes—three to Rice—that he started feeling sorry for Denver. "To have it go that well in a Super Bowl makes the game fun," said Montana, "but you get to a point when you start thinking about what it must be like to be on the other side."

The West Coast Offense

Bill Walsh often is credited with creating the "West Coast Offense," but the history of this unique offensive philosophy dates back to the San Diego Chargers teams of the 1960s, when Chargers coach Sid Gillman put five receivers into the offense. When Walsh worked as an assistant coach with the Cincinnati Bengals, he built on the idea of using more receivers on the field and giving the quarterback options for throwing either short or long passes. To succeed by using this offense, receivers had to be more durable and function a bit like running backs, sometimes making a short catch and then running through traffic. "We demanded that everyone be a good receiver and that everyone have great discipline," said Walsh. "I think those are still the foundations of the offense." In Cincinnati, Walsh put the system to use when backup quarterback Virgil Carter replaced injured starter Greg Cook. Because Carter did not possess Cook's arm strength, Walsh began using the offense, hoping that a 3-yard pass could turn into a 20-yard gain. Walsh then took his offense to San Francisco, where quarterbacks Joe Montana and Steve Young gave it greater fame.

THE OPTIONS BUILT INTO THE "WEST COAST OFFENSE" MADE IT SUCCESSFUL

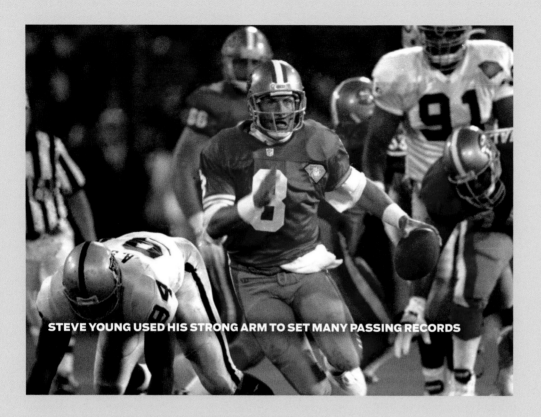

STEVE YOUNG USED HIS STRONG ARM TO SET MANY PASSING RECORDS

The Thrilling '90s

In 1990, the 49ers lost the NFC Championship Game 15–13 when the New York Giants kicked a game-winning field goal as time expired. The following season, Montana was sidelined by an elbow injury. Coach Seifert and the 49ers then looked to backup quarterback Steve Young.

Young had joined the 49ers in 1987 and remained in the background for several years, learning from Montana and waiting for his chance at the starting role. "When the opportunity opened up, being a regular quarterback was no longer an option," Young said later. "I had to rise to the new standard of performance that Joe set."

At first, San Francisco fans were skeptical of their new quarterback, but Young soon won them over. His physical talents were obvious: both fast and strong-armed, he could scramble to pick up extra yards and throw with tremendous accuracy on the run. He also proved he would do whatever it took to win, including taking big hits. "Of all the players I have coached or been around, Steve was perhaps the most driven athlete I've ever seen," said 49ers quarterbacks coach Mike Holmgren.

JERRY RICE'S PHYSICAL STYLE OF PLAY EARNED HIM AWARDS AND RENOWN

Joe Montana

QUARTERBACK / 49ERS SEASONS: 1979–92 / HEIGHT: 6-FOOT-2 / WEIGHT: 200 POUNDS

Despite leading his college team, the University of Notre Dome Fighting Irish, to a national championship during his junior year, Joe Montana was not picked by an NFL team until the third round of the 1979 Draft. Most scouts wondered if he had sufficient arm strength and whether he was durable enough to withstand the hard knocks of professional football. But 49ers head coach Bill Walsh recognized Montana's talents. "The minute I saw Joe move, there was no question in my mind that he was the best I'd seen," said Walsh. "I knew with the offense I planned to run, Joe would be great." Walsh was right. During Montana's years with the 49ers, he led his team to 9 playoff berths and 4 Super Bowl victories. In the process, he became a master of late-game comebacks, and his "Montana Magic" helped his team come from behind in the fourth quarter to win 31 times. Always even-tempered, he earned the nickname "Joe Cool" because he kept his poise so well under pressure. By the time he retired, he was only the fifth quarterback ever to pass for more than 40,000 career yards.

"PRIME TIME" PLAYED FOR FIVE NFL TEAMS AND FOUR MLB OUTFITS

Under Young's leadership, San Francisco's winning ways continued. In 1992, the 49ers went a league-best 14–2 before losing to the Cowboys in the NFC Championship Game. The following year, the 49ers went 10–6 and returned to the playoffs to face the Giants. In that game, 49ers running back Ricky Watters ran for five touchdowns, setting an NFL single-game playoff record and carrying the team to a 44–3 win. Unfortunately, the Cowboys again ended the 49ers' Super Bowl hopes, beating them 38–21 in the NFC title game.

Everything fell into place for San Francisco in 1994. Young embarked on one of his best seasons, throwing for 3,969 yards and 35 touchdowns. Rice set team records with 112 receptions for 1,499 yards and 13 touchdowns. The 49ers also featured a new star in lightning-fast cornerback Deion Sanders, known as "Prime Time" because of his clutch performances and love of media attention. A two-sport athlete, Sanders had once hit a home run for the New York Yankees baseball team and scored an NFL touchdown for the Atlanta Falcons in the same week. Wearing 49ers red and gold in 1994, Sanders made six interceptions and returned three of them for touchdowns, earning the NFL's Defensive Player of the Year award. Tackle Dana Stubblefield also starred on defense, netting 8.5 quarterback sacks.

The 49ers roared into the 1994 playoffs and finally beat the Cowboys on their way to Super Bowl XXIX, where they met the San Diego Chargers. On football's biggest stage, Young tossed a Super Bowl–record six touchdown passes to lead the 49ers to a 49–26 rout and win the game's MVP award. With a

Super Bowl victory under his belt, Young finally felt he had escaped the large shadow of Joe Montana. "I've got a monkey off my back at last!" he said.

The 49ers fought their way to an 11–5 mark and the NFC West title again in 1995. The defense—including cornerback Eric Davis and linebacker Ken Norton Jr.—was the team's strength, leading the league in defensive scoring and setting a team record for fewest rushing yards allowed per game (66.3). But the Green Bay Packers bounced the 49ers from the playoffs, 27–17. One year later, the same two teams met again in the playoffs. In near-freezing temperatures and pouring rain at Green Bay's Lambeau Field, the 49ers were plagued by turnovers and fumbles, losing 35–14.

In 1997, Steve Mariucci replaced George Seifert as San Francisco's coach and led

DEFENSIVE TACKLE BRYANT YOUNG (#97) BEGAN HIS CAREER WITH A SUPER BOWL WIN

Quarterback Controversy

When Joe Montana suffered a severe elbow injury and missed the entire 1991 season, the door swung open for Steve Young, Montana's backup of four years. Although Young had a good season despite missing five games with an injury, the 49ers missed the playoffs for the first time since 1982. With Montana due back in 1992, many people believed Young should be traded. The 49ers thought otherwise. Montana's injury proved more serious than expected, so Young remained the starter. He had an outstanding season and was named the NFL's MVP. Montana played briefly in the regular season's final game, and it was clear that he was fully recovered. Now the 49ers faced a dilemma—who would be the 1993 starter? Coach George Seifert said he couldn't keep Montana on the bench. Yet it would be difficult to do the same thing to the reigning MVP. The dispute spilled over into the 49ers locker room, with some players favoring Montana and others on Young's side. Montana supplied the answer, requesting—and being granted—a trade to Kansas City. The two teams met in the 1994 season, with Montana's Chiefs edging Young's 49ers, 24–17.

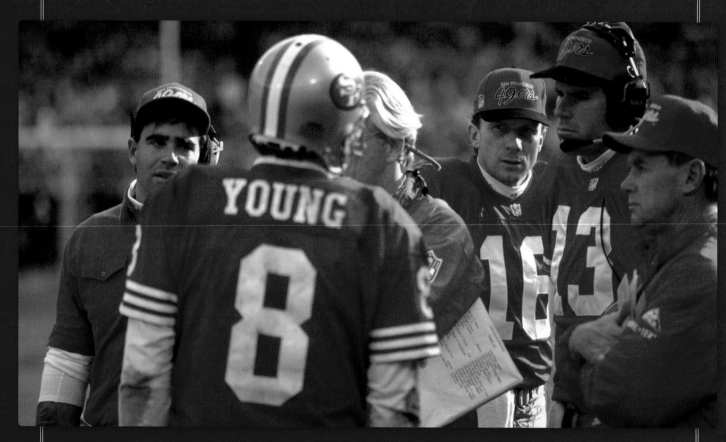

IT WAS DIFFICULT FOR MONTANA TO WATCH YOUNG TAKE OVER IN HIS PLACE

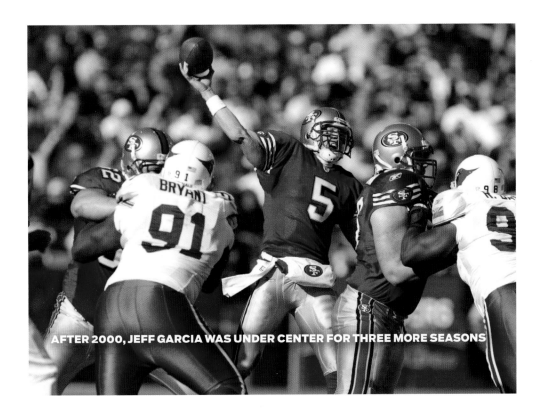
AFTER 2000, JEFF GARCIA WAS UNDER CENTER FOR THREE MORE SEASONS

the 49ers to an 11-game winning streak. Running back Garrison Hearst became the first 49ers player to rush for more than 1,000 yards since 1992. Knee injuries sidelined Rice for most of the season, but young receiver Terrell Owens picked up the slack with 936 receiving yards and 8 touchdowns. In the postseason, though, San Francisco again fell to the Packers, this time 23–10 in the NFC Championship Game.

The 49ers remained among the NFL's elite in 1998, racking up a 12–4 record and advancing to the playoffs for a rematch with the Packers. With only three seconds left in the game, the 49ers finally beat the Packers when Young rifled a 25-yard touchdown strike to Owens, bringing the final score to 30–27. The next week, however, Atlanta inched past San Francisco, 20–18.

In 1999, Young suffered his fourth concussion in three years and was lost for the season. San Francisco plummeted to 4–12, the club's first losing season in 17 years. Young then retired, opening the door for Jeff Garcia, a small but quick quarterback. Garcia proved himself a worthy successor by passing for a team-record 4,278 yards in 2000.

After posting 186 touchdowns and nearly 20,000 receiving yards during his 16-season career in San Francisco, Rice left town in 2000. Owens then became Garcia's primary target. With his 6-foot-3 and 230-pound frame and sure hands, Owens established himself as one of the league's best receivers. In a game against the Chicago Bears in December 2000, "T. O." pulled in 20 receptions, setting a new NFL record. "He's big, he can run, and if you play him one-on-one, he can outjump a defensive back," said St. Louis Rams defensive coordinator Lovie Smith. "He's the complete package."

TERRELL OWENS LED THE LEAGUE IN TOUCHDOWNS IN 2001 AND 2002

Fighting Back Up

After recovering from an ankle injury, Hearst returned in 2001 to rush for 1,206 yards and help the 49ers reach the playoffs. However, Green Bay once again knocked the 49ers from Super Bowl contention. In 2002, San Francisco returned to the playoffs to face the Giants. Although the Giants led 38–14 late in the third quarter, the 49ers charged back. During the last 17 minutes of the game, the 49ers executed the second-biggest comeback in NFL postseason history by scoring 25 points to win 39–38. However, the 49ers were unable to muster the same magic a week later, losing to the Tampa Bay Buccaneers, 31–6.

The 49ers dropped to 7–9 in 2003. Then, after Owens was traded to the Philadelphia Eagles, the team fell from the ranks of the contenders. In 2004 and 2005, San Francisco managed a combined total of only six wins. In 2005, the 49ers welcomed new head coach Mike Nolan, son of former coach Dick Nolan. Nolan looked for young players he could build around, and he soon found one. Despite splitting carries with fellow running

GARRISON HEARST RACKED UP RUSHING YARDAGE IN 2002 (WITH 972)

Ronnie Lott

CORNERBACK, SAFETY / 49ERS SEASONS: 1981–90 / HEIGHT: 6 FEET / WEIGHT: 203 POUNDS

After being selected eighth overall in the 1981 NFL Draft, Ronnie Lott immediately earned a starting role as a rookie. Known for his speed, strength, and knowledge of the game, he quickly became a leader among the team's defensive backs, a group that became the cornerstone of San Francisco's much-improved defense. Lott played a significant role in the team's overwhelming success during the 1980s. During his rookie year, he picked off seven passes, returning three for touchdowns. He led the league in interceptions twice, with 10 in 1986 and 8 in 1991. But Lott probably became most famous for his brutal tackles. "Nobody's ever tried to hit a guy harder than he does, and he does it on a regular basis," said Pete Carroll in 1994, then Lott's coach when he was with the New York Jets. Lott worked hard both on and off the field to improve his play, even studying martial arts to enhance his flexibility and self-discipline. A versatile player, Lott excelled no matter where he lined up. He received 10 Pro Bowl invitations at 3 different positions: cornerback, free safety, and strong safety.

back Kevan Barlow, rookie Frank Gore put in a solid first season in 2005, leading the team in rushing yards.

The 49ers improved to 7–9 in 2006, Gore's first season as a full-time starter. The 5-foot-9 and 215-pound halfback rumbled for 1,695 rushing yards, a franchise record. San Francisco ended the season on a high note, stunning the Broncos with an overtime victory that kept Denver out of the playoffs. "Beating a good team at home in overtime in a tough environment just shows the growth of this team," said 49ers wide receiver Arnaz Battle.

Although the 49ers entered 2007 with high hopes, injuries derailed the team's season. Rookie linebacker Patrick Willis shone brightly through an otherwise disappointing

FRANK GORE WAS A CONSISTENT WORKHORSE FOR THE 49ERS' OFFENSE

TIGHT END VERNON DAVIS HAD A CAREER SEASON IN 2009

5–11 season by making 137 tackles and earning NFL Defensive Rookie of the Year honors. Such efforts gave Bay Area fans reason to remain optimistic that the team would soon return to its former glory.

Those hopes didn't come to fruition the next few years. Mike Singletary, who had replaced Nolan as coach, lost his first game in 2008, but he endeared himself to fans when he said, "Our formula is this: We go out, we hit people in the mouth." Under his leadership, the team won five of its final eight games to finish 7–9. The 49ers improved to 8–8 the following year, their first non-losing season in seven years, and were a trendy pick to win the NFC West in 2010. But the club began the season 0–5 and never really recovered, finishing 6–10. Singletary, who sometimes got into sideline shouting matches with his players, was fired just before the final game.

The team didn't waste any time in finding a new leader. A few days after Singletary's departure, San Francisco hired Jim Harbaugh, a former NFL quarterback who had just led nearby Stanford University to national prominence during a four-year coaching stint there. As sportswriter Jason Cole noted, the 49ers were "going to play with all-out effort. For those who didn't get a chance to see Jim Harbaugh coach at Stanford, this is the same thing he did when he was there, and it has carried over to the 49ers."

The 49ers embraced their new coach and his methods in 2011, running away with the division title by assembling a stunning 13–3 record. One key to this amazing turnaround was the vastly improved play of

A Captain of a Coach

During his 14-year career as an NFL quarterback, Jim Harbaugh was known as "Captain Comeback" for his knack for engineering come-from-behind victories. The name also proved appropriate during his subsequent coaching career. After Harbaugh led the University of San Diego to back-to-back 11–1 seasons, Stanford University hired him to turn their program around following a 1–11 season in 2006. With Harbaugh on the sidelines, the Cardinals improved to 4–8 in 2007. They also earned a thrilling, 24–23 win over the 41-point favorite USC Trojans in one of the greatest upsets in college football history. Two years later, the Cardinals put a 55–21 beat down on USC en route to an 8–5 season. That set the table for 2010, when the Cardinals went 12–1 and narrowly misssed playing for the national championship. The 49ers then made Harbaugh their head man. Jim's brother John Harbaugh, coach of the Baltimore Ravens, praised the hiring. "No doubt in my mind he'll be successful," said John. He was right. In 2011, Jim nearly led San Francisco to the Super Bowl in his first season and made it all the way to the big game in February 2013—against his brother.

"CAPTAIN COMEBACK" ALMOST DELIVERED AGAIN IN SUPER BOWL XLVII

DEPENDABLE TACKLER PATRICK WILLIS WAS ALSO A THREAT TO INTERCEPT

43

ALEX SMITH WAS OFTEN INJURED AND SUFFERED A CONCUSSION IN 2012

quarterback Alex Smith, who had struggled since being the first overall selection in the 2005 NFL Draft. One of San Francisco's losses came in the "Harbaugh Bowl," in which the John Harbaugh-coached Baltimore Ravens knocked off the 49ers 16–6. The game marked the first time in NFL history that brothers had faced each other as head coaches.

After a first-round playoff bye, the 49ers hosted the Saints in a thrilling contest. The game pitted a fierce San Francisco defense against a high-powered New Orleans offense, and it featured four lead changes in the game's final four minutes. In the end, Smith fired a 14-yard pass to tight end Vernon Davis with 14 seconds remaining for a dramatic, 36–32 win.

Unfortunately, San Francisco's march toward the Super Bowl ended the following week with a 20–17 overtime loss to the eventual Super Bowl champion Giants. Two fumbled punt returns led to 10 Giants points that included the winning field goal. With Willis and end Justin Smith in place to anchor a stout defense, the 49ers looked to fortify their offense in the off-season, drafting quick running back LaMichael James and signing Randy Moss, who held nearly 20 NFL receiving records.

In 2012, the 49ers finished 11–4–1, barely held off a late surge by Seattle to win the NFC West by

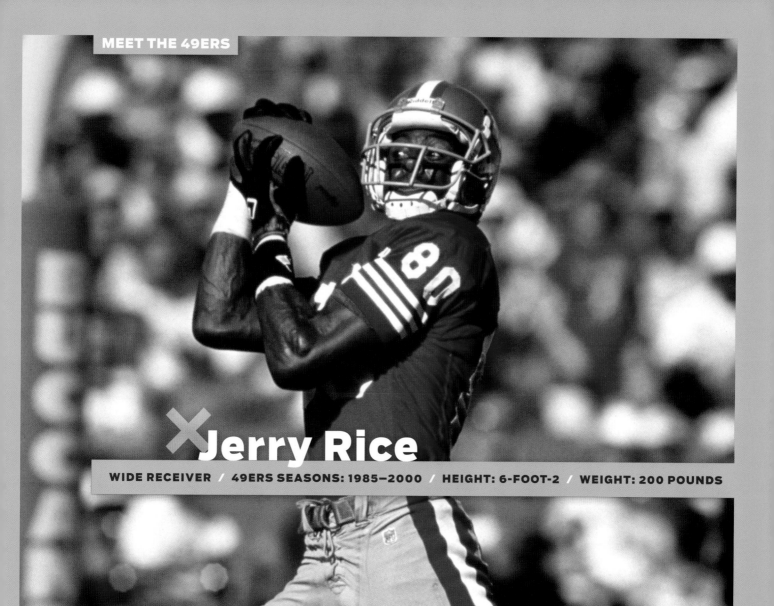

✕Jerry Rice

WIDE RECEIVER / 49ERS SEASONS: 1985–2000 / HEIGHT: 6-FOOT-2 / WEIGHT: 200 POUNDS

When the 49ers drafted Jerry Rice 16th overall in the 1985 NFL Draft, they hoped he would be a valuable addition to the team, but they had no way of knowing he would become one of the most prolific pass receivers in NFL history. In 1986, he led the league with 1,570 receiving yards and 15 touchdowns, but that was just the beginning. The following year, he topped the league with 23 touchdowns. Although he wasn't the fastest player in the game, Rice had deceptive speed that made him a threat to "go deep" on any play. Quarterback Joe Montana, who connected with Rice on 55 touchdowns for the 49ers, once said that Rice had a "knack for knowing when to break, when to use his speed." Rice worked hard, practicing drills as if they were real games and studying the methods of opposing defensive backs. He missed 14 games in 1997 recovering from 2 knee injuries, but he raced back to his record-setting form the following year, when he and quarterback Steve Young became the league's all-time top-scoring duo, with 80 touchdowns.

MICHAEL CRABTREE HAD A BANNER YEAR IN 2012, WITH 1,105 RECEIVING YARDS

JUSTIN SMITH HAD BIG HITS IN 2012, INCLUDING A SACK OF ELI MANNING

half a game, and suffered two blowout losses. Alex Smith suffered a concussion midway through the season that promoted second-year quarterback Colin Kaepernick to the starting position. Kaepernick soon developed a rapport with wide receiver Michael Crabtree, the team's top draft choice in 2009, who became a much more integral part of the offense. Kaepernick continued as starting quarterback, even after Smith recovered. "Colin, we believe, has the hot hand," Coach Harbaugh said. Kaepernick proved Harbaugh correct in the first playoff game. He outplayed Green Bay Packers signal-caller Aaron Rodgers, passing for 263 yards and a pair of touchdowns and rushing an NFL-record 181 yards. He remained poised in the NFC Championship Game as well, engineering a dramatic comeback win against Atlanta.

That set up the "Harbowl," otherwise known as Super Bowl XLVII, in which Jim Harbaugh's 49ers took on his brother John's Ravens. The Ravens took advantage of two San Francisco turnovers to build a 21–6 halftime lead and appeared to put the game away with a 108-yard kickoff return to open the second half. Then the lights went out—literally. A power surge darkened much of the Mercedes-Benz Superdome for more than half an hour. When the lights came back on, so did San Francisco's offense. At one point, the 49ers closed the gap to within 2 points, but Baltimore had just enough juice—stopping San Francisco 4 times inside the 10-yard line in the game's final moments—to hold on for a 34–31 triumph.

Throughout their long history, the San Francisco 49ers have rarely strayed far from contention, and with five Super Bowl titles, they are one of the most decorated franchises of all time. Today, thanks to their Jim Harbaugh-led resurgence, the 49ers are once again in the hunt for more golden Lombardi Trophies as NFL champs. It may well be that "The City" will soon host a championship celebration yet again.

INDEX